THE CHIHUAHUA SWAMI

First Printing: 2016
ISBN 978-0-692-62291-9
John Lucas/Fourth Chakra House
PO Box 25231
Winston-Salem, NC 27114
info@chihuahuaswami.com

www.chihuahuaswami.com

Ordering Information:
The Chihuahua Swami is available online at www.chihuahuaswami.com

Special discounts are available on quantity purchases by corporations, associations, educators, and others.
For details: orders@chihuahuaswami.com

Illustrations by Tiffany O'Brien
www.tiffanystarobrien.com

Thank you for adopting from a shelter.

THE CHIHUAHUA SWAMI

by JOHN MARK LUCAS

Fourth Chakra House

"Trying to not-love the world is exhausting."

PART I

THE CHIHUAHUA APPEARS

York County Animal Shelter
Pet Adoption Agreement
260 Public Works Rd., P.O. Box 120, York, SC 29745
Telephone (803) 628-3190 Fax (803) 628-3194

Shelter ID# 7-19-04-15 Pen 4   Date: 7-29-04

Name: John Lucas   Address: 120 N. Cedar St #3820

City: Charlotte   State: NC   Zip Code: 28202

Home Phone: 704 968 3748   Work Phone:

Type of animal: Dog   Breed: Chihuahua   Description: Tan

Approximate Age: ___ yrs. ___ months ___ wks. Male or Female

Pet's Name _____ Stray ✓ Owned _____

This pet received the following medical care:

(A) Rabies vaccination Date: _____ Tag #: _____ (D) FVRCP=Cat Distemper Combo Yes ___ No ___
(B) Worming medication Medication _____ Date _____ (E) Heartworm Check Date _____ NEG
(C) DPC=Distemper Combo Yes ___ No ___ (F) FELV/FIV Test Date _____ NEG

Name of Veterinarian: _____

PLEASE TAKE YOUR NEW PET TO A VETERINARIAN WITHIN 3 DAYS OF ADOPTION DATE FOR A PHYSICAL EXAM!

Important!! READ BEFORE SIGNING THIS ADOPTION AGREEMENT

1.) I hereby acknowledge receiving the animal described above.

2.) The animal listed above will reside at the address listed as adopter's address.

3.) I agree to have the animal surgically sterilized by 30 days / 3 months .

4.) To guarantee the animal be sterilized, I am placing a $ 50.00 surgical deposit with the York County Animal Shelter.

5.) The total dollar amount paid ($56.00) covers the cost of the sterilization and a rabies vaccination for the animal I have chosen. If the animal chosen has been spayed or neutered an adoption fee of the same amount still applies.

6.) I understand that failure to sterilize the animal and provide proof within the time period specified will constitute a default under this agreement, and The York County Animal Control shall be entitled to immediate possession of such animal and I shall forfeit all amounts paid to the York County Animal Shelter.

7.) I agree to license the animal in compliance with the laws and ordinances in force in the municipality in which I reside.

8.) The York County Animal Shelter is released from all liability once the animal leaves the shelter.

I HAVE READ THE CONTRACT AGREEMENT. I COMPLETELY UNDERSTAND AND ACCEPT THE RIGHTS AND OBLIGATIONS INVOLVED.

Signature of Adopter   Date 7-29-04

Signature of Staff   Date 7-29-04

CASH / CHECK / NC

Adoption Fee $ 50.00 Rabies Shot Fee $ 6.00 Total Fee $ 56.00 Receipt 66912

1

GOD REALLY IS DOG, SPELLED BACKWARD

Felix is a Chihuahua mix that I rescued from the jaws of death in 2004. He was in the York County, S.C. dog pound and less than 24 hours away from being put down. He had horrible kennel cough, several types of worms, you could see every rib and he was covered in fleas and ticks. It was a great first date.

Now once a dog entered the York County animal control system, it had only seven days to find a home. After that, it was killed. Felix had already been there a week. But since he was not violent or deathly ill, (he had a lot of issues for sure, but none of them deadly), they had kept him an extra week. But he was on the last day of his stay of execution.

For weeks I had been searching online for a Chihuahua. I didn't care what color it was, if it was male or female or how old it was. My only deal-breaker was that it had to be under the threat of death. Even though no-kill shelters and foster situations aren't the forever homes for animals, they are at least safe. So finding a dog that was in a kill shelter was a must.

My search had taken me to many websites, including Petfinder.com. There were plenty of Chihuahuas out there looking for homes, but each one I found was in a foster home or no-kill shelter.

But on July 29, I logged on at work and a Chihuahua that was within 100 miles of Charlotte, N.C., where I lived at the time, popped up on my computer screen.

I stared at his face and he stared right back at me. His name was "Ricky" and his expression said, "It's about time. I've been waiting for you to find me." I felt like I was moving in slow motion as I scrolled down to read his profile…

"…blah, blah, blah...*last day to adopt July 30.*"

(Sound effect: tires screeching to a stop)

Last day to adopt?

What did that mean? I'd never seen that on any of the profiles. Maybe they were moving him somewhere, to another shelter?

THE CALL

"Hello? I'm calling about a dog I saw online. A Chihuahua named Ricky? Do you know him?"

The woman on the other end seemed very business-like and a little short tempered, "What color?"

"Um. He looks tan."

"Chihuahua…tan…let me see…what's the ID number?"

"ID number? I don't see any ID number. His name is Ricky. It says he is at this shelter. Do you know him? It says the last day to adopt is tomorrow. What does that mean?"

"Means he's being put down tomorrow."

"What? He just showed up online today. I've been looking for weeks. Why? I don't understand. Do you know him? Is he there?"

I was beginning to feel a little desperate. My voice was inching up into tenor territory. My chest flushed with heat as my heart kicked it up a beat. I noticed my hand holding the receiver started shaking.

"How can you kill him? He just came online. I want to see him but I'm at work and can't get there. DON'T KILL HIM!"

"He's on schedule to be put down," she deadpanned.

"But he *just* came online. That's not fair. I can't get there today…"

"Tomorrow he's being put down. Is there another dog you are interested in?"

"No! My dog is Ricky! Ricky is my dog! You can't kill my dog!"

"He's not your dog sir. He belongs to York County. Get him today or you'll need to pick another dog."

I hung up. I was now ramped up to full-blown panic, and at work. Not a good combination. I looked up from my desk and over my cubical wall, scanning the office. I could see people milling around talking to each other, clicking on their keyboards, running off copies at the printer, dropping coins in the vending machine; but there was no sound. Everything was dead silent. Every once in a while someone would make eye contact with me and smile, or point to their watch to remind me of an upcoming meeting. But there was no sound. I was in a bubble. I felt disconnected from everything.

I knew I was at one of "those moments" in life. I had to make a decision. It was almost 2 o'clock. Ricky would be dead in a matter of hours if I didn't find a way to get to a dog pound in the next state before 5 o'clock. And I had a staff meeting in an hour.

4

I looked over at Scott, my co-worker in the next cubical. He was a dog lover and had a hyper Jack Russell (aren't they all?). I knew what I had to do.

"Scott." He had headphones on and didn't look up.

"Scott." Nothing.

"DAMN IT SCOTT!"

Scott, along with about 30 other people, looked up.

What happened next, I have to say, is unclear. It was like an out-of-body experience. I was looking right at Scott and could see him talking to me, but again, I couldn't hear anything. His mouth was moving, but what was he saying? I was motionless, just staring at him.

The next thing I knew I'm hearing the sound of my own voice, like it was walking in from another room, getting louder and louder as it got closer and closer. I realize I'm in mid-sentence telling Scott about Ricky. It was like I was coming out of a drunk's blackout. I'm not sure how long I had been talking or what I had said, but suddenly the silence bubble burst. All the office noise came pouring in and I hear Scott say, "Let's go."

Without missing a beat, with no thought of meetings or traffic or time, I grabbed my phone and told a co-worker I wouldn't be at the 3 o'clock meeting. Scott and I headed out of the office through the back door, high-tailed it to his car in the parking lot and hit the road for South Carolina.

To say that the pound was "in the country" would be kind. It took us over an hour and a half of winding two-lane state roads to find it. When we finally saw the sign, "York County Animal Shelter," I was shaking and almost in tears; probably a combination of way too much coffee, fear of losing my job, country-life phobia and general drama-queen tendencies.

As we drove down the gravel road, I saw several bunker-like cinder block buildings. Low and squat, with fencing up around them. It looked like a prison. As we got closer, I rolled my window down. The hot air, with vapor hits of mowed grass, animals, dirt and rain eased up my nostrils and calmed me down a bit.

Scott parked and turned off the engine. Immediately, nature turned up her volume. The sound I remember most was the locust. Loud. Really loud. Like a chorus of hysterical lawnmowers filling the heavy Southern air. And behind that sound, dogs barking, dogs barking, dogs barking.

There were a couple of workers walking around the buildings in county-issued green jumpsuits. "Killers," I thought. These were the thugs who were going to throw Ricky into a gas chamber along with hundreds of other poor animals. Dogs, cats, rabbits, pot-bellied pigs....the list is probably endless and includes animals I didn't even know ended up at the pound.

How do they do it? What are they thinking when they grab a dog or cat and lock them in the killing room? How can they do this every day? I was overwhelmed as I imagined what goes on at this place. Seeing it in my mind's eye. Hearing the howls and cries. I shut my eyes and let the locust chatter fill my head.

After a minute or two, I looked over at the driver's seat and realized Scott was talking to me.

"What?" I said, coming out of my trance.

"Are you ready to go get Ricky?"

"Ricky? Ricky! Oh my God. Ricky is in there!"

Scott and I jumped out of the car and headed toward the main building. The hot July afternoon mugginess hung in the air as mosquitoes bit my forehead, neck and hands. Temperatures were in the upper-90s and humidity was at 100%. It felt like we were walking through steaming pudding. The locust buzz was deafening and my skin seemed to vibrate with the noise.

We got to the door of the building and I stopped. Scott started to reach for the handle but I pulled his arm away. He looked at me and sensed I needed a moment. I needed to catch my breath. My thoughts were out of control. I knew something was about to change in my life. This had become something bigger than just adopting a dog.

I stood at the door, looking back toward the car, past the buildings, past the chain link fence, past the gravel road to the field beyond. The buzz in my ears transitioned from a frenetic, schizophrenic chaos to a monk's steady ohm. Somehow, it straightened itself out, like a traffic jam of honking cars all trying to get through a one-lane tunnel. Once inside the tunnel, there's order. The honking stops. The flow emerges. That is what I felt. The mad, desperate rush to find this place was over. I was here. I took a deep breath of the country air and smiled at Scott. We both knew it was time.

The front door opened directly into a small reception room. The walls were cinder block, painted light blue. One wall had a window that separated this main room from a small office area where a woman sat talking on the phone. The floor was that kind of polished granite that reminded me of the hallways of my elementary school. There were a few plastic chairs against the walls and a table with some old magazines. It was dated, to say the least. It felt like a doctor's office from the 1960s.

I walked over to the window. The woman on the phone smiled and motioned that she would be off in a minute. As I waited, I began to see details in the room I had initially overlooked. It was as if my vision was clearing up. I was focusing. What had seemed like clutter all over the walls, ragged pieces of paper with yellowed tape, began to take form.

They were pictures. Hundreds of pictures all taped to the cinder block walls. Dogs that had been adopted. Cats that had been saved. Pigs smiling back at the camera. Rabbits that were getting out of this place. Animals that knew what salvation was. Pets that were going home. And each picture had a hand-scribbled note with it: Jessie April 14, 1998; Barney December 23, 2000; Harry July 12, 1999; Skip, Stu, BettyBoo, Anchor, Bailey, Boston, Cherry, Gizmo, Coco, Dizzy, Zing-Zing. All saved. Maybe this place was not the killing ground I thought it was.

"Hello? Can I help you?" The woman behind the glass was off the phone.

"Hi. I'm here for Ricky. He was online. I called."

"Ricky? I don't know any Ricky. Is that a dog or a cat?"

I immediately panicked. HOW COULD SHE NOT KNOW RICKY!

With a wobble in my voice, I said, "I called. I spoke to someone. Did I speak with you? Did you talk to me on that phone? I asked you about Ricky A dog. He's going to be killed tomorrow! I have to get him! Ricky! Ricky! I have to get Ricky!

Clearly, I was off-the-rails again. This woman was going to cause me to collapse in a pool of sweat and tears right on the nice polished granite floor. But I'll be taking her down with me if she doesn't find me that damn dog.

The heightened volume of my voice echoed around the room. The dogs in the back started barking with more purpose. Did they recognize the ranting of someone who came to set them free? Were they calling, "I'm here! I'm here! Come get me!"

"Sir! Sir! You can't yell. Just tell me which dog you are looking for. When did you see it? Do you have the ID number?"

"Again with the ID number? No! It just said Ricky!"

Sensing my desperation, she tried to defuse the drama and explain to me how the online process works. "I need a number. Or a description. Those names are just given to the animals by the volunteer who adds them to the website. We don't have any names here. Please calm down. I want to help you. But I need you to tell me what he looks like and what the description said."

9

"He is going to be killed tomorrow. That's what it said. That's why I'm here." Then, in a quiet, hopeless voice, I said, "He's small. He's tan. He's a Chihuahua."

"I know him," she said.

My brain froze. My knees buckled. I grabbed the window counter and Scott grabbed me as I started to sink. The woman jumped out of her seat and disappeared through a door behind her.

Scott poured me into one of the plastic chairs. I looked again at the walls. Covered in adoption pictures. Covered. So many happy endings. Would my picture go up there? Would somebody, years from now, come in to save an animal and see a picture of a happy tan Chihuahua with yellowed tape holding it up?

The door in the little office opened and the woman stepped back into her room. She looked at me. I stared back at her. Why doesn't she say something? Why is she just standing there?

"They killed him!" I screamed.

"Can you come up to the window sir?"

"He's dead! You weren't supposed to kill him till tomorrow! I'm here for him!" My energy was gone. I said softly, to myself, "I came to get him…I called…"

"Can you come up to the window sir?"

Scott put his arm around my shoulder and walked me to the window. I was almost out of life force. I whispered, "Why? I came in time. Why did you kill him?"

"Ricky is not dead. He is waiting to meet you. They've secluded him off from the other dogs. I checked his record and he's been here two weeks. A week longer than usual, but he's non-violent so they kept him an extra week. But he'll be put down in the morning. He has some medical issues, but nothing life-threatening."

Scott grabbed my arm. I looked at the woman. She shuffled her papers, gingerly tapped them on the desk to get them in order and then looked at me and smiled.

"Let's go get Ricky," she said

THE MEETING

A door to the left of the window opened and the woman, whose name was Peg, motioned us through. Peg led us down a long hall with concrete floors, cinder block walls, heavy metal doors and bad overhead lighting. As we walked, she told us that Ricky would be in a pen by himself so the other dogs wouldn't interfere with the visit.

Dogs barking. Dogs barking. Dogs barking. Was Ricky one of them? Was he crying out to me, "Hurry, hurry!"

The walk down the hall seemed to take forever. At the end, another door. Peg fiddled with a huge key ring but finally located the one needed to unlock this barrier. I looked over at Scott. A trickle of sweat slid down from his hairline. It made me realize how hot it was in here. The building has no air-conditioning. It's stifling. How did I not notice this? Did Ricky have water? Were these animals, on death row, even given water? My thoughts were hitting a bottom. Would Peg just open the friggin' door.

Jingle, clank, gurrrrr. The lock moved and we headed into the holding area. This was the hard part. There were small pens, basically concrete pits, about four feet square, sectioned off with chain link fencing. Each pen had a dog or two in it and as we walked past them, they whimpered, barked, stood up and performed for me. Anything to get my attention. This was their final curtain call and they were doing all they could to find a home. I couldn't look at them. If I made eye contact I would only be telling them, "No." Peg, who was walking in front of us, turned around and motioned ahead a bit, "Ricky is up there. On the right."

Slowing down, I stared straight ahead trying to focus on the pen that Peg had indicated. As Scott and I walked up to the gate, what I saw took my breath away. There, in the middle of this concrete pit, stood a

 defeated, scrawny Chihuahua. He wasn't jumping or barking or trying to get my attention. He hung his head low and wouldn't look at me. As Peg unlocked the pen so Scott and I could enter, his eyes slowly shifted toward us, but he didn't lift his head.

Ricky was a short-haired dog who had been found wandering the streets of York, S.C., two weeks earlier. He was covered in fleas and I could see every one of his ribs. He had skinny, skinny legs and long, long ears. His nose was pink, but crusty.

I walked into the pen, with Scott behind me. Ricky didn't move. He just stood in the middle of this hot, smelly cell and looked down. His spirit was broken, and my heart was breaking.

Peg closed the gate behind us and I knelt down, not making any move toward the dog. Although Peg had told me that one reason they had kept him an extra week was because he was non-violent, I didn't want to risk getting him frightened and attacking in defense. Who knew what was going on inside his head?

I squatted on my knees like a catcher at home plate and opened my hands so he could see there was nothing in them. I saw Ricky slowly shift his eyes and stare at my feet. He wouldn't look me in the eyes. Then his head, just slightly, pulled up and he took in my scent. He was reading my intentions, sensing my motives and detecting any threat. He stood there motionless for another minute. I sat there motionless. Scott stood off to the corner.

Ricky and I just waited. Neither of us was sure of anything at this point. No rules. No expectations. No past and no future. This was uncharted territory for both of us. Another minute went by. A bead of sweat dropped from my chin. The other dogs were barking, still hoping, but the dingy pen I was in had become a sacred space and I couldn't hear anything except Ricky's breathing. I could sense what he thinking, deciding how he would play out this life and death game of chess.

Then he made his move.

Without lifting his head, he slowly walked the few steps that separated us. He entered the space between my knees, the open space that put him in "my" territory. With his head still hung down, he positioned himself between my legs, turned around slightly and looked back at those steps he had just taken. He gave a heavy, end of the world sigh, and then sat down and *leaned* into my leg. He never looked at me. He never lifted his head. My heart broke open.

With Ricky gently anchoring himself on to me, I looked up at Scott and then over at Peg. My mouth hung open; my jaw had gone slack. The three of us stared at each other, back and forth. No one was sure what to do. Scott and Peg obviously knew I had to take Ricky home, but it wasn't their place to say anything. So they stood stone still, to see how the next moment would unfold, what I was going to say.

"Let's get him out of here."

Peg broke down crying. Scott let out a soft whispered, "Yes."

I looked down at Ricky. He was still staring at the cement floor. I touched his head lightly and asked him, "Do you want to go home?"

Then, for the first time, he looked up. He looked up and right into my eyes. We stared at each other. It was really my first good look at him. His eyes were dark, hollow. His face gaunt, like he was starved. His ears, pink and crazy big. His legs were toothpicks.

"Peg, he's covered in fleas," I said.

"No problem. We can fix that." She left the cage for a minute and returned with a spray bottle of "something." She doused Ricky with the

concoction and immediately fleas and ticks dropped to the ground. It was like a magic act. I think it was kerosene. I don't have any proof, but that's what it smelled like. I imagine it probably stung, but Ricky just stood there. He seemed to know his fate had just changed. Mine had too.

That's the story of how Felix came into my life. His name change, from Ricky to Felix, happened fast. A wonderful friend at work decided that was his name. She said it meant "lucky."

Felix and I have now been together over 11 years. We moved from Charlotte, N.C. to New York City, where I had lived previously for 18 years. We've spent summers on Cape Cod and Fire Island, and in 2014 we moved back to North Carolina.

Over those years, Felix has had more than his share of medical issues. About 9 years ago he started to lose weight and became lethargic

It happened so slowly that I didn't notice the changes. But a friend who had not seen Felix for a while met us on the beach at Fire Island one day and looked at Felix and said, "John…what's wrong with Felix? He's lost so much weight…he looks sick."

I was dumbstruck. I looked at Felix and it was like I was seeing him for the first time. He *was* thin and looked tired. I bent down to touch his face and realized how fragile he was. How had I missed this? I scooped him up and ran back to where I was staying and packed a bag.

We caught the ferry to Long Island, the train back into Manhattan and then a cab to the vet. He was immediately given fluids and monitored for a few hours before the decision was made to transfer him to the emergency hospital on 5th Avenue.

Within an hour, they had him diagnosed with Addison's disease and started treatment. He was in intensive care and I was told that he was close to death. Again I asked myself, how could I have not seen this?

If Felix could survive the next 48 hours, then odds for managing the Addison's would be good. He did survive, obviously. But he spent five days in the hospital and I am still paying off that bill!

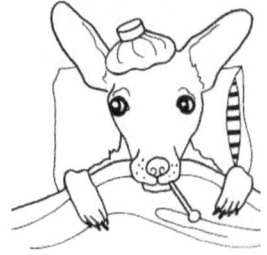

Since then, Felix has had severe gum disease and has only one tooth left in his mouth. Evidently, teeth kept Felix's tongue in place, because since his teeth were pulled, his sweet pink tongue often hangs out the side of his mouth. He's had seven bladder stones removed, had his gall bladder removed and is on medication for congestive heart failure.

But if you didn't know all that, you would think he is the picture of perfect health. He's bright, happy and performs his "circus dance" every evening when he hears the refrigerator door open and he knows it's time for supper.

PART II

THE SWAMI APPEARS

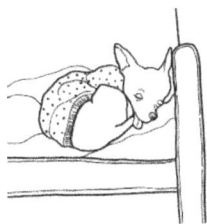

In March of 2015, I was sitting on my sofa having coffee and reading my daily *Course in Miracles* lesson. Felix was lounging beside me, his head resting on a pillow and his rear end bumped up to my hip so he could be sure I was there.

Author's confession: That's not exactly true. Felix was resting comfortably when I moved myself closer to him so I would be bumped up next to him. I needed to be sure he was there. I am completely co-dependent on this dog.

Anyway. In this story, we are both on the sofa. I am chugging coffee and he is minding his own business, sleeping. As I'm prone to do, I look over at him, and as usual, I see the most beautiful, kind, loving, giving, funny creature on earth. Ever.

I can't help myself. I have to put the coffee down and love on this dog. The moment demands it. How could I resist this warm baguette with a cold nose? His paws, the pads of his feet, *need* kissing. They just do. Don't ask.

So I give in. I lean over and smother him with affection. I rest my ear on his chest, listening to his heart, feeling his breath, in and out, as I think, "Is there anything in this world full of more love than this dog?"

I lie there for a minute, just sinking deeper into bliss. Felix rolls over, stretches and asks for a belly rub. I massage his chest and then slide my hand down to his back leg and scratch his hip. This causes him to extend that little leg out like a Rockette and I work my scratching all the way down to his teeny-tiny little toes and massage each one individually. And again, I think, "Is there anything in this world full of more love than this dog?"

After a minute I know I either have to get on with my day or just pull a blanket over both of us and give in to nap time. It's only 7:30 a.m., so to give in to the first nap of the day seems a little hedonistic, even to me, who's like a kindergartner that loves nap time.

So I reluctantly sit back up and tell myself I can't fold at this early hour. Felix gives out a little groan as his pointed leg relaxes and he lets his whole body return to resting mode. I gently lay a flannel over him, cause God knows I have to make sure this 11-pound-mind-controlling-reason-for-my-life-isn't-in-the-least-bit-uncomfortable.

I do know how ridiculous this sounds. I do!

After he is all tucked in, I just sit there and gaze at the perfection of this dog. One more time I think, "How could there be such a thing that has so much love? How could there be such a being that radiates love in everything he does? Every look he gives me, every paw he lifts, everything about him says I love you."

I stare at him. He lies there. I stare at him some more. He lies there some more. Then I have a mind-blowing experience.

As I look at Felix, I am aware of being filled with such love, such peace and such a sense of home and safety that it is almost overwhelming. I'm not sure if I've ever, in my whole life, been this swept away by the feeling of love. I sit and just drink it in, all these feelings that I'm getting from Felix. I lean back on the sofa, place one hand on Felix's hip and close my eyes. I am in love.

A minute or so passes and then I have a single, simple thought…

"He isn't doing anything."

The thought just floats across the front of my mind and then drifts on out the window. I almost don't even realize I've had the thought, until it circles back around for another drive-by.

"He isn't doing anything."

This time, I catch the last echo of the thought and it starts to reverberate in my brain, like background music, like a commercial jingle you can't unhear. Eventually, it starts to jockey itself into a better position to get my attention. The echo becomes less echo and more call to action.

"He isn't doing anything" becomes a chant that finally registers in my consciousness causing me to open my eyes and consider what it means.

"He isn't doing anything? *Who* isn't doing anything?"

I look down at Felix. Slowly, like molasses slowly, I realize *he* isn't doing anything. *He is actually not doing anything*, besides just lying there, breathing softly. His tongue, as usual, is hanging out the side of his mouth. Yes, he is perfection but...*he isn't doing anything*.

Then I think, "If he isn't doing anything, he's not radiating any of this love, happiness and peace I'm feeling. He's just lying there, asleep. And if he's asleep, he can't have anything to do with this love I am feeling, or this happiness I'm surrounded by or this peace that's overtaken me sitting on this sofa. So, where is this love, happiness and peace coming from?"

I can't take my eyes off Felix. His belly slowly rises and falls with each breath. Nostrils, dappled with moisture, expand a little with each inhale. An eye twitches, an ear flicks. But he is asleep.

I start to feel like my body is going numb. My feet get that tingling in them you experience right before they go to sleep. A warm sensation starts creeping up my back. It spreads across my shoulders and wraps itself like a snug turtleneck around my throat. My ears heat up and then, like slow motion fireworks, the heat releases into my brain. I feel like my head is filling up with warm chocolate syrup and I'm about to go under. As I sink into this luxurious pool, I feel safe, cozy, protected. I feel at home.

Once I am completely submerged, a shift in perception takes place and I find myself "inside" my body. It's like my body is a statue, a hollow shell, and "I" and something that is not "I" which I'll call "Thinking" are lightly floating around like feathers inside this container that is my body. Even though the "I" and the "Thinking" seem to be different "things," they also seem to be connected; "I" know what the "Thinking" is thinking.

(I know this is getting confusing, but try and work with me.)

I feel like I am in a calm, sweet and very loving presence as the "I" starts to unknot the knot of understanding where this love, happiness and peace is coming from.

The "Thinking" thinks, "It is obvious that Felix is asleep and is unaware of anything outside of his dream state. It is also clear that you believe the love, peace and happiness you feel is coming from Felix."

And then, from deep inside the space of my body, I hear, "How could Felix be responsible for anything if he is asleep?"

These words seem to hang in the air, waiting to be comprehended. "I" don't feel any stress or hurry or anything like this is a test of any kind. Everything is soft, patient and even helpful, if there could be such a thing as "helpful" in this place I find myself. As odd as it sounds, it is like a paper towel that has been laid over a wet spot. The paper just absorbs the water at its own pace, knowing that it's doing its job.

In this case, "How could Felix be responsible for anything if he is asleep?" is the wet spot, and I am the paper towel, taking it in.

Then, as if someone very quietly started to pull back a heavy velvet curtain, with a soft rustling I hear, *"He is not the love."*

The "me" that is floating around in the body stops aimlessly drifting and is drawn like a magnet to this idea, *"He is not the love."* It feels like an anchor or hitching post that "I" have tethered myself to.

The container, the hollow statue that is my "body" melts away, it just dissolves, and I experience how heavenly it is to not be limited by a body or any other defined space. I do not even have the concept of "beginning" and "end." The idea of "body" is gone and "I" am now simply the "Thinking."

"He is not the love" rises up again like a voice from the depth of this endless place and the "Thinking" that is now also the "I" thinks, "This has never occurred to me. I have always associated the love with the dog. I always felt that Felix was the source of the love, happiness and peace. Felix had become not just the object *of* my affection, he had *become* the affection. I thought Felix was the love."

There is a feeling of letting go, or release. "Expansion" is probably a better word, and I understand that Felix cannot be the source of these feelings. They are not coming from him. *All this love, all this happiness and all this peace is coming from me. It is coming right out of me.* Felix has nothing to do with it.

The heavy curtain now flings wide open with a snap, like a loud handclap! In a flash, this knot of understanding unties itself like a loose shoestring and instantly I am back "in" my body, sitting on the sofa. I open my eyes, blinking a couple of times like I am trying to get used to a new pair of glasses. Everything is blurry and the air in the room, the energy, is different. There's a vibration, like electricity, to the most familiar things. The lamp, the rug, my running shoes, everything, has a buzz that I can feel, like the locusts back in South Carolina.

Felix is still asleep. As if to drive home that point, he starts to snore. His little back legs start to kick like he is having a "running" dream. But he is totally unaware of me or that I am awash in love, happiness and peace.

I sit quietly, knowing any movement will interrupt the download I am getting. Some kind of gate has opened and I can see how this understanding about myself and my feelings doesn't just apply to how I feel about Felix. It applies to every single thing in my life. Nothing comes from the outside. Nothing comes from anyone or anything else. Everything comes from me. No one else is responsible for what I feel.

I am aware that I am having some kind of creative mind shift. This is a new way of looking at life and how to operate in the world. And Felix is sleeping though the whole damn thing, as usual.

My couch-potato-reality-blip doesn't last long. It's like *boom, sizzle, fry, done!* After about 10 minutes, I wiggle my toes. The moment seems to be over. It feels like I have been very far away and that I could have been gone a second or I could have been gone a year.

My consciousness seeps back into the room and I start to feel physical again. To say the least, I am at a loss for words. I don't know what to do. It is clear to me that I have just had "a moment," but what do you do after a moment?

My instinct tells me to write this down. I have a terrible memory and need to write down anything I really want to remember. So I reach over, get my journal and start writing.

The process of writing is helpful to me. When I am not writing, my thoughts are a jumble of ideas and broken links. But writing sorts and filters everything down so I can keep on one trail and finish to the end. I've had wonderful insights while writing that I would never have discovered on my own. What I wrote about and finally got to is this:

I am the love.

That's it. That is the simple truth. All the love that I thought was coming from Felix? It's coming from me. It's my own doing. Felix may be my muse, my touchstone, but he is not the energy that is flowing through my body coating every cell with peace, charging every nerve with happiness and filling every emotion with love. That is self-created. I am capable of that. It's an inside job.

And the next part of this truth is a doozy: If I am the love, *then I am also the "not-love."* What is "not-love"? It's obvious isn't it? It's everything that is not love.

LOVE & NOT·LOVE

Felix showed me the source of all the love. It isn't outside. It isn't a person. It isn't an amount of money. It is right here, sitting next to the Chihuahua. And by showing me the source of all the love, he also showed me the source of all the not-love. Not-love can look like hate, anger, impatience or anything else that is not love. That source is also sitting on the sofa.

Here are two examples of my not-love in action.

My not-love gets triggered when I am waiting in a checkout line and I think the clerk is too chatty or too slow or just not doing her job like I think she needs to do it. My body language projects my internal thoughts of not-love. To the outside world, it may look like impatience, but now I know what it really is. First I'll give out a big sigh. If the clerk doesn't catch my drift, I'll add some foot shuffling and maybe pull out my phone to look at the time. Next, another big martyred sigh. Finally, I'll just drop my mouth open, stand akimbo and stare at her. It's a performance that, if I observed someone else doing, would make me laugh. But Felix has opened my eyes to its true nature. It's not impatience; I am expressing the hostility of not-love and the clerk is completely innocent. Even if she *is* slow and not paying attention to her work, she is not the source or even the cause of my behavior. She is neutral. I am the not-love.

Another one of my big not-love temper-tantrums happens when I am at a stoplight and the driver in front of me is texting and doesn't go when the light changes. I admit it, I go crazy. I lay on the horn and cuss in my head, if not out loud in my car.

OK, he *is* texting. But he is not this rage I feel inside. He is totally neutral. He is texting, and that's what he is doing. All this anger? That's what I am doing. I am lost in my not-love. Lost.

It's difficult to put into words what I felt as I sat on the sofa and the truth about the source of love made itself clear to me in no uncertain terms. It's a "knowing" that can't really be written down — it doesn't involve words. It's a mystic experience because "knowing" is not physical and "love" is not physical. I can't box "love" up and give it to you. I can't put it in a card and send it in the mail. Sure, I can have sex and call it "making love," but is it really? Nope. Sex is just a physical expression, a symbol of a feeling I have; but presents, cards, sex and Felix are not the love.

When I really got grounded in understanding that Felix was not the love, I have to admit that I felt I was being unloving toward Felix. I'm not saying I felt like I didn't love Felix, not at all. I'm saying I felt guilty that I was somehow not loving him as much. Like I was taking something away from him and reducing his value by seeing him as neutral. It was an uncomfortable feeling, but at my very core, I knew I loved him even more. Felix had in fact become my teacher. He had become my beloved Chihuahua Swami.

However, I did have to ask myself how in the world could I actually think that Felix was the *source* of the love, happiness and peace that I was feeling? All I can say is, "I did." It never, ever occurred to me that he wasn't. I grew up with animals and have had them my whole adult life. And each and every one of them produced the same feelings I was having with Felix. No one ever told me that these loving feelings I felt with my dogs and cats were coming from me.

Now, I get it, you're sitting there thinking, *"My God John, why would someone have to tell you that? It's obvious."*

My response is, "No, it's not." I ask you, when you were a child, did a parent or teacher or friend ever sit you down and point blank say, "Listen kid, I want to tell you how your emotions and feelings work"? No one did that with me. And in fact, the outward projection of internal thoughts and emotions onto things and people is a common psychological pattern of behavior. So growing up, I projected those feelings of love, happiness and peace that I felt with my pets, *onto* my pets. To me, it was as natural as associating the feelings of love I felt for my parents with the physical form of my parents. They were the love I felt. No doubt about it. As a child, I felt love when they were in the room. When they left the room, I felt the love was gone. When they came back in the room, I felt the love again. So of course I would think that they were the love. But the truth is, they were symbols of my own natural capacity to love.

And speaking of symbols, I want to say that my talking Bugs Bunny stuffed animal, my Easy Bake Oven, several Hot Wheels cars and a certain Dr. Seuss book were also sources of love I felt as a child. I tell you this because it makes it clear that anything can seem like the source of love, or not-love.

Now it's easy (for me at least) to see how an Easy Bake Oven can be the projected source of love. But you may be wondering how the heck can an Easy Bake Oven be the source of not-love?

So let me tell you a story…

Once upon a time, a little boy (me) got exactly what he wanted at Christmas: an Easy Bake Oven. Now that little boy had really campaigned for that oven. He wrote to Santa, including a cookie and reindeer treats in his letter. He prayed for it in Sunday School. He told his parents and teachers about it and described everything that came with it. He cut pictures of it out of the Sears catalog and had them in his pockets at all times. And come Christmas morning, Ta-da! The little boy ran downstairs to find that Santa had carried an Easy Bake Oven on his sleigh all the way from the North Pole.

Now next door lived a Grinch. He believed that boys should only play with trucks, Army action figures and baseball gloves. On Christmas morning, Grinch (who was not celebrating Christmas you know) heard the shriek of excitement the little boy let out when he saw the Easy Bake Oven. Grinch slowly peeled his black curtains back just a sliver (curtains were drawn tight of course) and peered into the window of the house next door. "What is all this laughter and hugging about?" he growled deeply to himself.

Surveying the scene, Grinch's eyes spied the little boy setting up his Easy Bake Oven and mixing cake flour in a bowl. The boy was experiencing profound love at this moment. While at the same time, Grinch grew deeper in contempt and hate and everything else that is not-love. He decided then and there that

Easy Bake Ovens were terrible and were ruining little boys across the land.

For the remainder of Grinch's days (which were friendless and never included cake) all of his darkness was projected onto the Easy Bake Oven. Whenever the sweet smells of baking from next door drifted into the cold rooms of his house, Grinch's thoughts of not-love, in all their variations, were triggered. This caused his heart to beat wildly against his chest (i.e. heart attack), his fingers to form fists that became knotted and stiff (i.e. arthritis) and his insides to gurgle and boil (i.e. irritable bowel syndrome). While all around him, love was waiting to be inhaled with the next breath.

It's a silly little story, but it does illustrate how love and not-love can be projected onto things, ideas, concepts, nations, people and even Easy Bake Ovens. And don't miss the real point of the story: the Grinch may indeed live next door, but he most certainly lives much closer. He lives right inside you and me. He is the not-love.

IRONIC IDOLS

The list of what I project not-love on to is endless and includes people, places and things. But it doesn't stop there. There's another non-physical layer of not-love projections that goes even deeper. These are the beliefs, hurts, resentments and justifications in my life that I've held on to for years. They are the cancers that will eat away at me over time. They will become my heart attack, arthritis and irritable bowel syndrome.

The truth about these beliefs, hurts, resentments and justifications—these things I think I hate—is ironically the complete opposite of what I've always thought it was. In reality, all these hates are actually my true loves, my idols. *Why else would I hold on to them for so long?*

My Chihuahua Swami showed me that these resentments, prejudices and my darkest beliefs are indeed my most cherished possessions. I worship them by nursing them, keeping them alive and making sure they are never healed.

I'm not a "religious" person at all, but I did grow up going to Sunday School so I am familiar with a few of the Bible's concepts and passages. In one of the "commandments" it says to not put any idols before God. I think that perfectly addresses this idea of how I love my resentments, hates, hurts and grudges more than my wanting to heal them. They are my blocks to the awareness of love.

THE HEART

My heart is a big pumping power plant and my thoughts are the coal being shoveled into my heart's furnace. When I hold on to resentments, hurts and anger, refusing to let them heal, then I have a *heart condition*. I could call it many things, a weak heart, a heart attack, a bum ticker, but the bottom line is, these unhealed, heavily guarded, negative, not-love globs-of-plaque are my very personal attacks and defenses against love.

According to centuries of Eastern thought, the heart, or the fourth chakra, is where the physical and the spiritual come together, or where heaven and earth meet. I see this as the place where the Chihuahua

31

Swami has led me. When I am able to let my earthy, physical life and my spiritual, non-physical life flow together, then I am balanced, or in harmony.

It's really kind of simple. When I am experiencing the body's thinking patterns of hate, justification, rage and the long list of other not-loves, then my heart tightens up, beats with irregularity or not-love energy, and sends that energy to every cell in my body, causing physical, mental and spiritual imbalance.

But when I remember the love that Swami Felix showed me is always accessible, always right inside me, my heart opens up, radiates warmth and circulates positive healing energy, or harmony, to every cell.

That harmony is what love feels like in the body. That's the feeling I experience when I look at Felix or, when I was a child, the feeling I had when I saw my Easy Bake Oven on Christmas morning.

There's a passage in the Bible that poetically talks about this, or at least that's how I interpret it:

> *When I was a child, I spoke as a child,*
> *I understood as a child, I thought as a child;*
> *but when I became a man, I put away childish things.*
> *For now I see through a glass darkly.*
>
> 1st Corinthians 13, verse 11 and 12

What this tells me is to never lose my love for Easy Bake Ovens. I bet you didn't know that! It's true. If, as an adult, I lose my inborn childlike innocence and openness and capacity to speak with love, understand with love, and think with love, then I will see the world darkly. I become the Grinch: isolated, cold and viewing the world from behind my heavy curtain of not-love.

That morning on my sofa, the Chihuahua Swami opened my eyes and my heart by showing me that all the love in the world is a choice, and it is as close as my next breath. I just have to be aware of my thinking and pay attention to what my heart is telling me. Am I in harmony? Are my heaven and earth energies balanced? Is my heart circulating love or not-love? If it is not-love, then I have a *heart condition*. If it is love, then I am *in love*.

TAKE A BREATH

Breath is an amazing tie-breaker. When I am in that space of choosing to react with love or not-love, a few breaths can throw the contest to love's side. It can stop the not-love train right in its tracks.

Breath is a pause in reaction. It's like a comma in the sentence of whatever is going on.

Felix has shown me that even when I am *in* the not-love, right in the thick of it, the healing is still as close as my next breath. Breath interrupts, on the spot, my thinking pattern. It can slow down, or even stop, knee-jerk reactions, anger, physical impulses and other not-love actions. When I breathe in, I'm not pulling something in from the outside for a quick fix. I'm pulling the healing up from my own source. *The quick fix is in me.*

When I remember to call up that love that is in me, I am working with the power I need to heal those cherished idols of resentment, hurt and justification. Felix showed me that everything is my own doing and un-doing at the same time.

WHAT IS LOVE?

Love is organic. I didn't invent it, build it or buy it. It was born with me. So when Felix made me aware that it is always in me, I had to ask myself, "What *is* love?"

I knew it was a feeling. I knew it made me want to be nice. I knew it made me kinder. But what exactly *is* it? Well, that stumped me.

This seemed to be such an important question. If something made me feel so good, why didn't I know what it really was? Why isn't someone packing it up and selling it?

And right there is part of the answer: because love is not a commodity. Contrary to what I see on TV and in magazines, I can't buy love. It ain't for sale. This makes sense to me, but it only tells me half the story, it only tells me *what love is not.* I still needed to know *what love is.*

In my search for the answer, I remembered three words from the Bible, "God is love." Well, this seemed to be answering the question, but backwards. I didn't ask what God was, I asked what love was. But whatever. The definition worked for me.

Question: What is Love?

Answer: God is Love.

Not only did this answer my "What is love?" question, it also cleared up the mixed emotions I've always felt about "God." It's hard not to have some preconceived idea of God. For me it was always an old white guy in the clouds. Someone very far away and who was pretty judgmental and a little fickle. I mean, he's supposed to be my "father" that loves me, but he's also going to smite me with just the wave of his hand if I eat clam, crab, lobster, mussels, oyster, scallop, or shrimp. That seems a little trigger happy to me.

So by bringing together what the Chihuahua Swami showed me, *that love comes from inside me*, and what the Bible says, *that God is love*, I decided that *God must be that feeling of love inside me*

I am overjoyed by this idea of what love is and what God is. It makes sense to me. But even more, it feels right to me. It clarifies God for me and it makes it a very personal experience. God is that love that Felix showed me was inside me. God is not "he" or "she" or some Supreme Judge or a "being" at all. God is Love.

Now when I read something or hear someone talk about God, I just automatically substitute the word Love. And I capitalize the "L" because it's like a proper noun. It changes everything. Love is something I can work with. Love is something that seems gentle and kind. Love has no trigger-finger and certainly doesn't smite.

The Swami has taught me all this. He has given me an understanding of God *and* Love. That is no small feat. And he did it while taking a nap. Is that an enlightened master or what?

THE NOT-LOVE STOPS HERE

Felix taught me that he is not the Love and neither is anything else out there. Everything I see is a reflection of what I am thinking at that moment, Love or not-love. If I blow my top in traffic and think the guy in the next lane is a jerk, the Swami simply asks me to remember that the driver is a jerk if I think he is a jerk. If I see a jerk, then I can take a breath and untie the knot of not-love. Or is that knot-love? When I *remember to remember Love*, then the driver is a driver. Nothing else.

Seeing something with Love doesn't mean I am always happy or approve of what I see. Not at all. There's nothing happy about a flat tire and there's nothing approving about war.

Seeing whatever is going on with Love just means that I catch what I'm thinking, and if it's not-love, then I silently or out loud just repeat, "I Love you. I Love you. I Love you…"

I say it over and over and over and over and over and over and over. It's important for me to remember that I am not saying "I Love you" to try and convince or trick myself into believing I don't have negative thoughts. It's not like I'm saying, "I love you flat tire. I love you war."

When I'm saying "I Love you," it's a mantra that will, if I let it, *eventually* cause me to interrupt the negative not-love thoughts about flat tires, war, checkout lines, traffic and everything else.

"I Love you" becomes an action word, like a verb. A verb sentence, if you will. With "I Love you" I am throwing a bucket of Love onto whatever issue or problem I have or can see. Think of it like Dorothy, in *The Wizard of Oz*, when she throws the bucket of water on the Wicked Witch of the West. The Witch is the not-love and the water is the Love. Love melts not-love. Love always wins.

With "I Love you," I throw Love around, where previously I would have thrown not-love around. *I am reversing the dynamics of my life right there on the spot.*

So what about the horror and tragedies of life? What if I'm crippled with fear? What if my life is actually falling apart? Am I able to gloss over everything and just hum, "I Love you?"

I doubt it. Odds are very good, in fact I'd bet on these odds, that "I Love you" is not going to be my first response. But at some point, it may be seconds later or it may be years later, I will choose to work on whatever horror or tragedy I've experienced, with Love. Unless that is, I love it so much that I want to keep the hurt, resentment and anger alive and unhealed.

I have been that unhealed person, many times. *I've held on to the stories, my idols, that have identified me to me for years.* My not-love has been relentless at times and has caused me to keep the pain of my past alive in my present. This prevents me from experiencing Love, peace and happiness today. It causes me to not-love my life and that causes me to not-love my world.

And trying to not-love the world is exhausting.

When I decide to use Love to heal my past, at that moment, I change history. I see my past differently. I see it with the power of Love. And when I do that, *I also change the history of my future.* When I don't drag not-love from the past with me, it can't be a part of the rest of my life.

I have come to understand that my only real block to ongoing Love, peace and happiness is thinking that Love is not the answer to everything. When I believe that, I block Love and I experience what *A Course in Miracles* calls the separation from God.

But when I do practice Love with all things that come up in my life, *all things*, then I am connected to "God" and I am living in Unconditional Love

UNCONDITIONAL LOVE

When I live my life, with all its joy and pain, while practicing "I Love you" with everything, *one thing at a time*, then I am living in and with Unconditional Love.

For me, the "one thing at a time" is key. It would be too unrealistic to pretend that I could say "I Love you" once and mean it for everything for the rest of my life.

I know some people say *that's* true unconditional love. But that seems way too big for me, at least for today. If I tried to live like that I'd fall flat on my face, and that would probably make me feel like a loser and failure most of the time. I don't think my Swami would want that.

What works for me is practicing "I Love you" on things as they come up, or as they say in AA, one day at a time. And some things just keep coming up, over and over. So I continue practicing "I Love you," pouring it out until I feel my heart shift from not-love to Love. For me, Unconditional Love means that there is nothing in my world that, at some point, I am not willing to meet with, "I Love you."

SELF LOVE

The Chihuahua Swami has shown me that I am the Love and that the not-love can stop right here. This Love that he has opened my mind to changes everything, by changing the way I think about everything. This Love is extremely personal. Another name for it is *Self Love*.

Self Love is that organic Love that was born in me.

Self Love is that capacity to speak, understand and think with Love.

Self Love is nothing short of a revolutionary way of living.

Self Love is not learning to love yourself — Self Love is learning that your Self is the Love.

STARVE A COLD, FEED A FEVER

So where has all this Swami Love led me? In a word, "farther." It has taken me to a place that, along with *A Course in Miracles*, gives me a way to look at the world with a macro and micro lens.

I don't think I am alone in feeling that the world seems to be spinning off her axis with a jumbo dollop of crazy on it. The fear, hatred and selfishness are sicknesses at epidemic proportions.

But! At the same time, there is a spirit *fever* that has spiked around the world. I personally feel this fever, and I'm sticking with the "starve a cold, feed a fever" cure.

The Chihuahua Swami made it clear that I am going to see, experience and then tell the story of whatever I choose to think. When I look at society, governments, churches and whatever else you can throw in there, and think any piece of it should live by my rules, my opinions, my beliefs or my fears, then I become the terrorist. I demand the world work my way, and if you think it should work your way, then I attack. Sometimes the attack is outward, and sometimes the terrorism is in my own mind and I become the terrorist and the victim.

A Course in Miracles says that everything is "either an expression of love or a call for love." So I choose to feed that spiritual fever in myself and *try* to answer all the judgmental chatter, negative blaming and hate speech in the world and in my head with "I Love you."

Hello crazy driver: I Love you.
Hello politician: I Love you.
Hello co-worker who can't do anything without help: I Love you.
Hello sickness: I Love you.
Hello disease: I Love you.
Hello terrorist: I Love you.

Remember, saying "I Love you" is so you don't lose your connection with God/Love in any circumstance. If we lose that connection, then we enter the battle that is fought outside the mind, where there are no winners.

Never forget…
When I think that Love is not the answer to everything,
I lose my connection to God/Love.

About the author

John Mark Lucas was born in 1959 in Shawnee, Oklahoma. His family moved east, to Winston-Salem, NC in the summer of 1967.

John received a BA in painting from Guilford College in Greensboro, NC. In 1983, he moved to New York City where he got his Master's Degree in painting from New York University.

In 1985, a friend handed him a copy of *A Course in Miracles*. Unable to grasp the concepts at the time, he put the book down until 2004. Since then, he's been a dedicated student and teacher in both New York City and North Carolina.